Writing 23

By Robert Creeley

ROBERT CREELEY

The Charm
Early and Uncollected Poems

Four Seasons Foundation

San Francisco: 1969

Grateful acknowledgment is made to the following publications in which most of these poems first appeared: *Accent, The Beloit Poetry Journal, The Black Mountain Review, Burning Deck, Chelsea Review, Contact* (Toronto), *The Floating Bear, Four Winds, The Free Lance, Fuck You/A Magazine of the Arts, The Galley Sail Review, Goad, Golden Goose, Gryphon, Hearse, Mica, The Naked Ear, Nomad, Origin, Pegasus, Poems from the Floating World, Poetry, Poor. Old. Tired. Horse., Wake* (also *The Harvard Wake*), *The Window, Yugen.* Acknowledgment is also made to the Golden Goose Press for the poems printed in *Le Fou*, to Divers Press for the poems in *The Kind of Act of* and *A Snarling Garland of Xmas Verses*, to Vincent Ferrini for the poems in *Ferrini and Others*, to Jonathan Williams for poems in *The Immoral Proposition* and and *All That Is Lovely in Men*, and to Corinth Books and Jonathan Williams for a poem in *A Form of Women*.

The majority of these poems were first collected in two limited editions, *The Charm* and *Divisions*, designed and printed by Walter Hamady and published by the Perishable Press Ltd.

Library of Congress Catalog Card No.: 68-57711

Cover photograph of Robert Creeley at Black Mountain College February 1956 by Jonathan Williams

The Writing Series is edited by Donald Allen
and published by Four Seasons Foundation
Distributed by Book People, 2010 Seventh Street,
Berkeley, California 94710

Contents

Preface

The poems in this book begin at the very beginning so to speak—"Return" was the first poem I remember having published, and was written on my coming back from India to Cambridge in the winter of 1945—and continue to a time which would include the writing of many of the poems in *Words*. Why there are this number, I don't altogether know. When *For Love* was first a possibility, I lacked copies of many of the earlier small books I had published, and had none of the manuscripts, so that I was dependent on texts such as *The Whip* (effectually a *selected poems*) and *A Form of Women*. Consequently I depended on the poems I had literally in hand and could not reconsider others I had cut from previous collections for whatever reason.

However, one poem—the title poem of this book, first published in *The Kind of Act of* in 1954—continued to stick in my head for many years indeed. The 'tongue' of that poem is still the one I am given to speak with. More I *like* this poem—in that it has continued to speak both for and to me, for all that time.

When I first began writing, I was very didactic and very involved with 'doing it right.' There was so much then to qualify what was acceptably a poem, and what was not. For example, there is a lovely story told me by John Frederick Nims about a friend of his reading somewhere in the Midwest. At the end someone in the audience asked if questions were permitted, and being told they were, said that he had one concerning the next to last poem read—to wit, 'Was that a real poem or did you just make it up yourself?'

In any case, whenever there was a chance to publish a small pamphlet or book, my temptation was to cut from it any poem that did not seem to me then and there to make adamant sense as a *poem*, and consequently I tended to ignore a kind of statement in poetry that accumulates its occasion as much by means of its awkwardnesses as by its overt successes.

One time in conversation with Allen Ginsberg late at night, when we were both in Vancouver in 1963, he very generously said to me, you don't have to worry so much about writing a 'bad' poem. You can afford to now. I don't know that my nature will ever allow me that understanding, which has not finally to do with some pompous self-regard—but rather with the fact that we are human beings and do live in the variability of that order. We don't know all we think we do, nor would it even be very interesting if we did. Another friend, Robert Duncan, has always insisted, with high intelligence, I think, that poetry is not some ultimate preserve for the most rarified and articulate of human utterances, but has a place for *all* speech and *all* occasions thereof.

Let me be, then, as gullible as obviously I once must have been, and enjoy the fact of having written these poems—which I know I did then, just that to be given to write anything is always pleasure. Selfishly enough, I can often discover myself here in ways I can now enjoy having been—no matter they were 'good' or 'bad.'

July 21, 1967

The Charm

return

Quiet as is proper for such places;
The street, subdued, half-snow, half-rain,
Endless, but ending in the darkened doors.
Inside, they who will be there always,
Quiet as is proper for such people—
Enough for now to be here, and
To know my door is one of these.

greendoon's song

it's the greyness said greendoon
bids the several of our clan
seek forever for a man
to put music in our tune

it's the brownness turns the leaf
sets us searching while we can
up and down the stranger land
for a single honest thief

it's the blackness of our grief
brings us back into the room
puts the lock into our hand

poem for d. h. lawrence

I would begin by explaining
that by reason of being
I am and no other.

Always the self returns to
self-consciousness, seeing
the figure drawn by the window
by its own hand, standing
alone and unwanted by others.
It sees this, the self sees
and returns to the figure
there in the evening, the darkness,
alone and unwanted by others.

In the beginning was this self,
perhaps, without the figure,
without consciousness of self
or figure or evening. In the
beginning was this self only,
alone and unwanted by others.

In the beginning was that and this
is different, is changed and how
it is changed is not known but felt.
It is felt by the self and the self
is feeling, is changed by feeling,
but not known, is changed, is felt.

Remembering the figure by the window,
in the evening drawn there by the window,
is to see the thing like money, is to be

sure of materials, but not to know
where they came from or how
they got there or when they came.
Remembering the figure by the window
the evening is remembered, the darkness
remembered as the figure by the window,
but is not to know how they came there.

The self is being, is in being and
because of it. The figure is not being
nor the self but is in the self and
in the being and because of them.

Always the self returns to, because of
being, the figure drawn by the window,
there in the evening, the darkness,
alone and unwanted by others.

poem for beginners

. . . and I could see in the clearing
beside the axe and the tree   (fallen)
I'd cut before dinner   (morning)
a squirrel and I ran for . . .   (problem)

So that one who has come back in passion
may sit by the other who has not left
and turn to this one and explain
what has happened and remain with it
unexplained; so that the other may sit
and return with this other in passion,
come back and remain unexplained;
so that each, together, may sit
and together each may, together, explain
and remain; it is, perhaps, necessary to complain
that it is passion which does this, does not explain.

—If you will follow this road as far as
the turning, you will come to a barn
with a red roof and a large silo.
If you ask them there, they should know
(i.e. they'll tell you where you want to go.)

Because, more than anything, it is the road
and its turnings that is the traveler,
that comes back and remains unexplained
and even sits in the doorway and looks over

the hills and sees sunsets and calls you
to see them too; because it is the road
that the returned one has traveled who
travels, who goes and comes and remains;
perhaps it is the road who can, perhaps, explain
that it is the passion which does this, does not complain.

—She was coming over before breakfast
to tell you herself but then she remembered
she'd told Judy and all the rest
of them that she was going to make bread
(because she didn't believe what he'd said
until the morning and the somehow unfamiliar bed.)

If, then, the problem is the road
and the passion we call traveler and one
who has remained; if it is to blame one
for coming or going, remaining or staying the same
or, perhaps, for not explaining or, better,
for not complaining; is there a name
for it? What is there, after all, to explain?
That passion is wild, the road runs, the traveler
has come back and sits and talks and goes again[
Perhaps it is the road and passion which complain
that it is the traveler who does this, does not explain.

. . . and I could see in the clearing
beside the axe and the tree   (fallen)
I'd cut before dinner   (morning)
a squirrel and I ran for my gun.

sanine to leda

Beyond this road the blackness bends
in warmth. Two, then three or four,
lovers with wisdom for themselves
enough are sitting there in vague,
unbending poses. They sit.
The quiet grass holds roses.

Begin with that. The beautiful
comes later. Love, the several roses,
lovers with wisdom for themselves,
vague, unbending poses. Look.
Each loses what he chooses.

the late comer

(parvenue) delinquent, who will now
guess that this, that this is you,
as if a delinquent, a late sorrow
had arranged this, being better
this way, being better late than

never,

for (believe me) there are still
flowers there, though wilted, there
are still flowers, as if there are
their flowers and wilted, their
sorrow, delinquent, as if in cool

weather.

It was never this or that they
wanted, so given their sorrow, or
was what they wanted yours and
would you have given them over
the flowers, the coolness, delinquent . . .

(better)

gangster

he said, turning, unconscious of
emphasis, why—goddamn it—I
was almost a gangster! Could
shoot straight. That's it. So
at morning, coming alone and
walking five miles, he could see
the horns and waited. Looking.
Until it was all there. He fired.

Simple? How simple? To say what's
what takes how much? Three cans
in a row, from the hip yet. No
joke. But to worry, to think
of it that way (the gangster)—
to see yourself like others
see you, Jesus, what pride!

Quieter, a wife and two children,
he'll wait for a reckoning.

11

poem for bob leed

O and we sang then whose voices
loud long-echoed so that the many
trees could not surround them and
we sang the warm songs the graceful
expositions the particular songs
and O the woods echoed what we sang

It is the long road he is coming
where dust all day rises and the sun
at noon is darkened with dust and in
the dry mouth the water is brittle,
tasteless. It is the day he lives
and the long road, dust-driven, no
stranger but who's all alone here
where he is, is coming tomorrow.

From windows, fresh curtains which smell
good and the hand that holds them there's
a stranger but none who could know it
and whose house is, what house is, now
a question, whose and tomorrow's
a day of dust and the road is another's.

What would it now take, another, a question
like others to answer, what now could
take him in, one bed for a stranger, long-
limbed and once handsome, who's ready to try

for the particular, adequate lover? Tomorrow
he'll die and be dead and whose bed will be
empty? One word, whose word, could be said.

but O and we sang then whose voices

from pico & the women: a life

Love God, we rather may, than
either know Him, or by speech
utter him . . . Disuse, good father,

these things have rusted and
we know a man who speaks more
freely of these and other, of

all wonders. We have hands,
now, and can hold all wonders.
And yet had men liefer, good

father, *by knowledge never find,*
good father, *that which they*
seek . . . These words are twisted.

°

Today is a green day. Today
we are away from those involving
questions, that the gods have

put upon us, wittingly, to bind,
to fetter, and surprise. And
the god's eye is clear, is an

unsurprising blue, with which
we are each familiar. We are
born to blue, under, god's lid,

good sky, blue sky, with which
we are each familiar. We are
born to sky, under, god's eye.

o

He will be sleeping somewhere
else, little rabbit, in the long
grass, in the hole of his own

making. He will be sleeping and
it will be our fear that lies
so. It is not our time nor our

spirit, but we will come to it.
It is our lion of fire, our
triumphant animal, with his own

victories, our hearts' conquesting
beast, little rabbit, that will
not bite you nor otherwise harm.

to the one in the gray coat

To the one in the gray coat,
sitting as though he were
asleep, were beyond these
involving actions, I will
address myself. Olé!

He will become conscious,
so, of the south. I have
called to mind for him,
have suggested by language,
a world of inner warmth,

a south of the spirit in
which he will be the one
who is not asleep, who
dozes in the completeness
of things which are warm,

in the sun, in the sun's
completeness. And the coat
as remnant, to be left on
the bench. And he will
know this and will leave it.

Then, going, he will have
passed me, in chill air,
the disciple, to say more
of, to go on with these
signs of inadequate love.

the epic expands

They had come in a carriage (which
will be less than what's needed)
over the hard roads. And they stop
in the town to get coke, three
bottles, by way of a celebration.

So will the epic expand (or be
expanded by) its content. So will
words throw (throw up) their meaning.
Words they have used (will use) are
the sound (of sound), what gets us.

But to go farther (he could not
stop there), to look at the old
people, graceless and cold, in a
carriage with only one blanket
between them, to keep out the cold—

and it was, he said (he said), it
was a coldness of the mind, too (too).
Yes, poets, we had overlooked an
essence, and quiet (put back into
quiet), we let the tears roll down.

love

The thing comes
of itself

        (Look up
to see
        the cat & the squirrel,
               the one
torn, a red thing,
       & the other
somehow immaculate

still life or

mobiles:
  that the wind can catch at,
against itself,
   a leaf or a contrivance of wires,
in the stairwell,
to be looked at from below.

We have arranged the form of a formula here,
have taken the heart out
    & the wind
is vague emotion.

To count on these aspirants
these contenders for the to-be-looked-at part
of these actions
   these most hopeful movements
needs
a strong & constant wind.
    That will not rise above the speed
which we have calculated,
   that the leaf
remain
  that the wires
be not too much shaken.

helas

Helas! Or Christus fails.
The day is the indefinite. The shapes of light
have surrounded the senses,
but will not take them to hand (as would an axe-edge
take to its stone . . .)

It is not a simple bitterness that comes between.
Worn by these simplicities, the head
revolves, turns in the wind but lacks
its delight.

What, now, more than sight
or sound could compel it, drive, new,
these mechanics for compulsion

                                       (nothing else but
to bite home! there, where
the head could take hold . . .)

                                       which are vague,
in the wind,
take no edge from the wind, no edge
or delight?

guido, vorrei che
tu e lapo ed io

Guido,
I would that you, me & Lapo
                    (so a song sung:
                    sempre d'amore . . .)
were out of this
                had got to the reaches
of some other wood.

Deadness
          is echo
deadness is memory
                    & their deadness is
petulant, the song gone
dead in their heads.

Echo
      is memory
and all that they foster
                    is dead in its sound
has no ripeness
could come to its own.

Petulance
          is force so contested.

They have twisted
                    the meanings & manner
the force of us out of us
left us the faded
                    (Who made musick
the sound of the reaches
                    the actual wood

hart crane 2

Answer: how old
is the wind, shakes the trees & moves with the
    movement of
(what is
       sound

I am again, and no more than
it was
      when the wind, when the trees, what
(is the sound of
         sound

(Sd he: the miracle
is it not, in our bath
like a lump of sugar
we don't dissolve
          (makes incorporeal even
their lightest phrase)

So sound is, was (apocryphal) the sound of
sound
    (what love
        apolaustic
           had broke this thing

littleton, n. h.

Day/
    diminutive

Night is the Mother, is the
Fixer of Change.

From which, from out of which
the Mind can take its center.

                    The Moon
as, say, round & inconsequent (Shine on

They say here, that, for change: the (4)
quarters of this most luminous moon
(now) must each be taken. Like
(not to be laughed at) the quarters
of a pie (or where the dollar goes . . .), it is
the graph, the locus of change.

Impossible (it is) for the stranger
to ever get these facts. He wanders alone here, finds drift & satisfaction equally off & away from him.
There was that road
turned off from the main one
to end in the backyard.

Now, (sua culpa) Kenneth stands in the corner
and remarks the cloud drift from
the third corner of
                    (not the room but) life.
His moon is the shade of the moon in the corner
of his room
                    (where it makes: the Sign

canzone

as would any sound make
more music
          than this scraping
his violin is not love
is not even love lacking
a purpose or an object for
its love

     (is not even sound
since sound has a shape in
the ear and this has no shape)

or
him & his violin

love

Not enough. The question: what is.
Given: grace
                the time of this moment
which I do not see as time.
The particulars: oak, the grain of, oak.
And what supple shadows may come
to be here.

Tell me something I don't know.
Of love, and I hear it, say:
speak to me, of love . . .
                                The crouched hand.
The indefatigable.
                        But quicken, but be
the quick!

. . . *the stain of love is upon the world!*

Which I have not written.

the festival

Death makes his
obeisance:
>   to the two
first, children. The wall
falling, to catch them and then
another, the aunt aged 6
also.

the surf: an elegy

Relative to cost, the high figures
of production:
                    you, sweetness & light
are destructive only in your
inveterate tendencies.

The poor are poor. The statement
the little people would not
I think
accept, is

that there is any refuge
that there is anything to be gained
in too simple formulation.

Or what else to destroy them with?
To keep them you, lover
grant is impossible:
                    the blot
is nationwide, the indulgence
federal.
            Dams, projects of even
immense size
take on but
a few.
            (But you are restless, the tide
pulls out, leaving scum, the likewise restless
and improbable
stores of the sea.

the drums

how are you harry the
last time we met it was
in heaven
surely
or so I remember

the sea

the wash, the plunge
down
        (saying:
we will not become you, we
are the impenitents
                        (the tears
We declare

the cantos

To make peace (borso
with the others,—or not too
quickly, give in to the companionable
ecstasy.

And she said, madame
your child speaks
french, whereas
previously
he could only hear it & we thought
understand.

A triumph. But dwindles quickly.
Since last fall he spoke it, I
had already
been proud, but not to her
of whom he had been frightened.

What to think of the dullness
of the provincial lady?
Not to think of it, we make
no makeshift adjustments
to the inadequacy
of anyone.

something for easter

I pulled the street up as you suggested
—and found what?
                    1 nickel
                    2 pieces gum
etc.

But we are practical
—but winter is long & however much one
does save, there is never
enough.

divisions

Order. Order. The bottle contains
more than water. In this case the form
is imposed.

As if the air did not hold me in
and not let me burst from what-have you or inveterate
goodwill!

To make it difficult, to make a sense
of limit, to call a stop to meandering—
one could wander here

in intricacies, unbelted, somewhat sloppy.
But the questions are, is it all there
or on some one evening

will I come again here, most desperate and all questions,
to find the water all
leaked out.

2

Take it, there are particulars.
Or consider rock. Consider hardness not as elemental but as
stone. The stone! And just so
invincible.

Which is to say, not a damn thing but
rock. But, just so, that hardness, which is to say:
the stone.

Or if only to consider, don't,
Loss exists not as perpetual but, exact, when the attentions
are cajoled,
are flattered by their purport or what they purport
to attend.

Which remains not, also not, definition.
But statement. But, very simply, one, just so, not
attend to
the business not
his own.

the question

A description of the sensuous
is its own answer: a multiple love is
mine.
      These women.

Who in their beds, their
beds or buttocks bared for the nocturnal
revels, agh!

Or if her tits be rose, or roses, or any
flower, with what, say, to water this
garden of particular
intent?

a poem

If the water forms
the forms of the weeds, there—

a long life is not by that
a necessarily happy one.

My friend. We
reckon on a simple

agreement,
the fashion of a stone

underground.

the mirror

When I see you in the first light, again
at the angle of the bed, in a light seen

face, and hand, hair. The horrible
incompetence, and dull passive greyness
of myself.
                    In disuse, and there is no use
got by nothing, and no competence
enough to make enough—

It becomes the incredible in which I believe,
that any god is love.

a variation

My son who is stranger
than he should be, outgrown
at five, the normal—

luck is against him!
Unfit for the upbringing he would otherwise
have got, I have no hopes for him.

I leave him alone.

I leave him to his own
devices, having pity not so much that he is
strange

but that I am him.

2

Myself, who am stranger
than I should be, outgrown
at two, the normal—

luck is against me.   Unfit
for the upbringing I would otherwise
have got, I have no hopes.

I leave him alone.

I leave him to his own
devices, having pity not so much for
myself, for why should that happen

but that he is me, as much as I am him.

two ways of looking in a mirror

At midnight the world is a mediate
perspective.
                        And hence
to an immaculate
bed, the time of

passion,
flower of my mind. Consumptive
prayers keep us: the moon in its low chamber.

And about us, rayed out in a floral wall-
paper-like pattern, the

facts of our union. Bliss
is actual, as hard as
stone.

medallion

Light, a form, a
shadow at the edge of the window, a

sullenness comes over me, un-
repentant.

What if the others don't care, what
is it you want
               (Lacunae

"flesh
of another color, a

whiter hand, with narrow, arching
fingers

old song

Take off your clothes, love,
And come to me.

Soon will the sun be breaking
Over yon sea.

And all of our hairs be white, love,
For aught we do

And all our nights be one, love,
For all we knew.

in an act of pity

In an act of pity your hands
are quietly offered, and are held at arm's
length, because they would be gentle.

Because I am not gentle my voice
is harsh, and my hands likewise. Because
I have nothing for you, and am wrong.

So it is to be wrong. To be at a loss
and unhappy, which is this loss
of one's happiness, in one who had held it.

the charm

My children are, to me,
what is uncommon: they are dumb
and speak with signs. Their hands

are nervous, and fit more for
hysteria, than goodwill or long
winterside conversation.

Where fire is, they are quieter
and sit, comforted. They were born
by their mother in hopelessness.

But in them I had been, at first,
tongue. If they speak,
I have myself, and love them.

the bird, the bird, the bird

for Charles

With the spring flowers I likewise am.
And care for them. That they have odor.

We are too garrulous (Brugm. i. § 638), we
talk not too much but too often.

And yet, how otherwise to oblige the
demon, who it is, there

implacable, but content.

a ballad

We have a song for the death in her body
and if the night is long
or the blackness blacker,
then something is effected from us.

But if, without hope, there is crying
and a moaning, a retching,
and the time is horrible,
and she cries and tries to escape from us—

do we then sit down with petulance
and a show of hate, and not like her?

for an anniversary

Where you dream of water
I have held a handful of sand.

My manners are unprepossessing.
I stand here awkward, and a long time.

I am mainly an idiot.
You are almost beautiful.

We will both be miserable
but no one is damned

47

los guitaristas

The music is a dance
for the ones who don't dance, it is

a wiggle, obscene, beginning with the
hips, and ascending forthwith

to the mind.

thank you

o Kindness, Kindness. These virtues are
for you pleasure, such

a radiance
of smiles, such

redundant satisfaction.

I am held by my fear of death

I am held by my fear of death.
I am deadened with it.

The thing in my hand is impassive
and will not

give me time. It is gone
and again I am

useless, impotent,
and the hell is potent

though I will not give in to it.
There is nothing beyond it.

the method of actuality

                                    the
mother (mother) unbent to give to
anyone.
                    The young
The sudden & inconsequent. The gentle
stare. I see myself in long & uncombed hair

bedridden, sullen, and face to face, a face of hair.
My mother's son.

the pedigree

Or if I will not rape
my own daughter
                    "What will I do?"

What, of what occasion, is not so
necessary, we do not
                    "witless"
perform it.

                    Or me.
Who am of common stock.

it is at times

als kleine begrüBung auf unserem
alten kontinent die paar zeilen

Of them, undefined
repetitions, the
inactual

      Lost, or spared
by the inaccurate, there
miscounted

        As of those lists
(the names)
repeated, the names
lost

    (As of an evening, talking
lost in
reflections, the

golden bowl

the europeans

Or me wanting another man's
wife, etc.

                    History.

Unable to keep straight
generations.

Telling them all about
myself.

the penitent

These, the unequalled, vicious
beyond even
love (who act on it, there pulled to
a variation

cruel even, but at least of
the senses

But upon that corpus
who is of that, flesh of

Or why else turn to it, pathetic
hopeless to avoid or caught even as were
the penitents, pants down.

eros

Also the headache of
to do right by feeling
it don't matter, etc.

But otherwise it was one, or even two
the space of, felt

and one night I said to her, do you
and she didn't.

for martin

In the narcotic and act
of omniscience

a gain, of the formal,
is possible.

Time is the pleasure.
Forget all the diversities & digressions.

Love tonight for the mind
and the body together. Be relentless

that our ugliness
be inhabited.

the trap

On a theme fantastic, a light
aria, by some altogether monstrous woman in
black tights,

the heart revolves itself,
congests, and tired,
lies to itself

again tired. Fastens
on sentiment.

the revelation

I thought that if I were broken enough
I would see the light
like at the end of a small tube, but approachable.

I thought chickens laid eggs
for a purpose.

For the reason expected, a form occurred more
blatant and impossible

to stop me.

an obscene poem

The girl in the bikini, my
wife, the lady—she sits on
the rocks, crouched
behind a jagged encumbrance.

Calamares, canalones—
the fisherman's daughter.
At night a dull movement
on the sands

and lightly at low tide
on the rocks
bland, undulant
she returns.

chasing the bird

The sun sets unevenly and the people
go to bed.

The night has a thousand eyes.
The clouds are low, overhead.

Every night it is a little bit
more difficult, a little

harder. My mind
to me a mangle is.

hi there!

Look, love
        ○ ○ ○ ○ ○ ○
            (oo)
                    springs
from out the
        ○ ○ ○ ○ ○ ○
            (oo)
            ()
                    surface of a pedestrian
fact, a new
        ○ ○ ○ ○ ○ ○
            (oo)
            ()
            (----)
                    day.

sopa

That old black goober that I ate
for lunch. Something in the bowl it was,

at the edge, up-
ended. Like when one

cracks one
peanut, how ever

to throw it away how-
ever dusty?

the changes

People don't act
like they act
in real life
in real life. They

are slower
and record the passive changes
of atmosphere.

Or change themselves
into green persian dogs
and birds.
                    When you see one
you know the world is a contrivance.
It has proverbiality.
People are poor.

for irving

At seventeen women were strange & forbidden phenomenons.
Today they leer at me from street corners. Yet

who is to say it,
that we have come to an agreement.

Aging, aging, even so there is some song, some
remote pulse,

an argument still visible, an
excuse for it.

broken back blues

O yr facing reality now—
& yr in the same beat groove—
you try to get up—
& find you just can't moo-oove
                    (take it take it
uncle john
we can play it all nite long . . .

        I got them things in my head—
no sounds will ever solve
                    (heh heh heh, heh heh heh . . .)

So yr bent in yr middle—
yr face is on the floor—
they take a great big club—
& beat you out the doo-oor
                    (watch it watch it

mr man
we're going to get you if we can

        that I'm alive today, I want to say, I want to say—
that I'm alive today
                    (heh heh heh, heh heh heh . . .)

I havent got a nickle—
I havent got a dime—
I havent got a cent—
I dont have that kind of time
                        (all rite for you, friend
                        that's the most
                        we herewith
                        propose a toast:

It's a hopeless world.

the happy man

Who would love you
if you were not six

feet tall, a ruddy face, a
smiling face. You

would walk all night, all
night, and no one, no one

would look at you.

for somebody's marriage

All night in a thoughtful
mood, she

resigned herself to a
conclusion—heretofore

rejected. She
woke lonely,

she had
slept well, yet

because of it her
mind was clearer, less

defended—
though confident.

stomping with catullus

1

My love—my love says
she loves me.
And that she would never have
anyone but me.

Though what a woman tells
to a man who pushes her
should be written in wind and quickly
moving water.

2

My old lady says I'm it,
she says nobody else cd ever make it.

But what my old lady says when pushed to it,—
well, that don't make it.

3

My old lady is a goof at heart,
she tells me she loves me, we'll never part—

but what a goofed up chick will tell to a man
is best written in wind & water & sand.

4

Love & money & a barrel of mud,
my old man gives out for stud,

comes home late from his life of sin,
now what do you think I should tell to him?

5

We get crazy but we have fun,
life is short & life gets done,

time is now & that's the gig,
make it, don't just flip yr wig.

the apology

I think to compose a sonnet
on ladies with no clothes. A

graciousness to them
of course.

for a friend

You are the one man
coming down the street on

a bicycle. And love is a certainty
because it is sure of itself.

The alphabet is letters,
the muskrat was a childhood friend.

But love is eternal,
and pathetic equally.

the total parts of a world

The form of the grasses against
the water is reminiscent, a total reminiscence
of the water in motion

and love itself a siren, a total
image.

Who is more unhappy than I am.
The voice wails. We

listen in unhappiness,
in love.

alba

Your tits are rosy in the dawn
albeit the smallness of them.
Your lips are red and bright with love
albeit I lie upon them.

And hence the grossness of the act
reverberating ever
reinstitutes the virgin ground
of body and of fever.

an irishman's lament
on the approaching winter

Hello to you, lady,
who will not stay with me.

And what will you do now for warmth
in a winter's storm . . .

A cold wind take
your mind from its mistake.

now then

When love is for-
bidden, it

is the most!
says Huggi Baba, an old

egyptian? Perhaps an
old man already at the time

of this pronouncement, when
love is forbidden.

trees

What shall I do with my friends,
if they won't answer my letters—
or if I make a joke, would it be better
not to send it to them?

This morning, clutching a daffodilly,
I sang of what things I could,
I would do better if I could. What would
make it all less silly.

Tonight when the goddess invokes me
with her back to me, would it do
to kick her too? Or should I tell it to you,
so that she will respect me.

I think: poets live in a well,
from whence the screams issue,
a fearsome hole it is too,
a very hell.

"to work is to contradict contradictions, to do violence to natural violence . . ."

To consummate
the inconsummate, and make of it

the unending. Work,
work, work.

Six days of the week you shall work,
on the seventh you shall think about it.

'Mary, pass the potatoes' becomes
division of subject & object.

Work, work, work.
Get them yourself.

Thought is a process of work,
joy is an issue of work.

not again

Sometimes I am embarrassed
by the recurrence of that pronoun
which calls into question, rather into
prominence, my own face.

Of course I
am embarrassed, what else?
Like with the waiter with the tray on which
repose (only) his own hands.

Always—
SundayMondayTuesdayWednesdayThursdayFriday
    Saturday—
no matter where I look,
I am there.

It was a breeze and a seashell
brought in Venus—
but I can be here
without going anywhere.

So goodbye
until we meet again,
and when you come, walk right in.
It's I.

the prejudice

There is a despair one comes to,
awkwardly, in never having known
apple-breasted women.

But that time was inapproachable
when I was younger
and now am older.

O is that destiny,
she said to me.

'you've tried the world, try jesus'

We laughed when he sat down at the piano
and it melted all over him.
We laughed later at the stew
we ate him in.

We laughed on the way home.
At that point he was inside us.
But now we are crying
and God won't hide us.

for a screaming lady

Pumping away pumping away
now everyone is pumping away.

The blood is circulated through the body
by hope faith and charity.

Big bands are assembled on every street corner
no one is crying anymore.

Now likewise when you see me you can look at me
because I won't be.

the picnic

for Ed and Helene

Ducks in the pond,
icecream & beer,
all remind me
of West Acton, Mass—

where I lived when young
in a large old house
with 14 rooms
and woods out back.

Last night I talked
to a friend & his wife
about loons & wildcats
and how to live on so much money per month.

Time we all went home,
or back,
to where it all was,
where it all was.

the menu

"John and I have decided
we do not like Al Haig . . ."

(Julia Wasp)
with applesauce

and pork
where there is smoke

there is desire
where what is true

is always true
I wouldn't like him either.

in a boat shed

I waited too long,
I waited for you forever and ever:

the changing unchanging restlessness
of the signs they didn't put up

or down; the boxes of oranges,
rat poisons, barns, a sled with no runners,

snow, refreshments, pineapples;
the odor of burnt wood, cigarettes

neither one of us should smoke,
but do—

I waited for you.

swinging down central

No matter what color my pants are
you are all in it together!
I don't want to go home.
Let me out let me out let me out.

Saturday was payday.
I keep saying. Pay me today.
I want my money
and want it now.

This night is love
night saturday dreams of
tokens of farewell on to
another's surprise surprise.

I should have died when I was seven
or eight or ten.
I should have been dead then
to have lived so long.

je vois dans le hasard
tous les biens que j'espere

When you said 'accidental'
I thought it was that you were formal
and sat down.
When I went home I did not
go home. You said
go to bed, and sleep, and later
everything will be clear.

It was a lovely morning yesterday
and I think things have at last happened which will not go away.

the herd

Way out they are riding, it is an old
time's way to continue to succeed
in recorded passionate hoofbeats,
animals moving, men before and behind them.

the door

Thump. Thump. The door
which never is knocked upon but cries,
for who sings, dies,
what goes, will go on.

nathaniel hawthorne

Hippety hoppety down
and there they are

heppel's wait's father
uncle jim is

stone face
is the legend.

the dream

A lake in the head
wherein they put a boat,
two trousered men
with four legs between them.

The women
go in swimming
in the nude.
They blossom into lewd.

That light shut off,
he rolls over
and under,
begins to smother.

the hands

Take the hands
off of
it and throw
them so that
they re-
occur, else-
where on
some other
woman.

the passage

What waiting in the halls,
stamping on the stairs,
all the ghosts are here tonight
come from everywhere.

Yet one or two,
absent, make
themselves felt by that,
break the heart.

Oh did you know I love you?
Could you guess?
Do you have, for me,
any tenderness left?

I cry to hear them,
sad, sad voices.
Ladies and gentlemen
come and come again.

what's for dinner

Only from the back
could I be seen clearly,
merely the fragment
into space hanging.

John jumped on Tuesday.
We had a date
but I was late, and he unduly
unruly.

Today my time come, I
am hung from this 7th story downtown window
to say hello
for the last time.

the animal

Shaking the head from
side to side, arms
moving, hanging as the
sign of pride,

mouth
wide open
to eat the
red meat

in the jungle,
in the heat.
But I am
not animal,

move,
discontinuous, on
two remote
feet. Then

it spoke, then
hair grew, and eyes,
and I
forgot my-

self—oh
no, oh not
(they say)
this like

an animal
he eats, and looks
like an animal
at us. It

spoke. Who
said it
could not, who
did not know.

the sentence

There is that in love
which, by the syntax of,
men find women and join
their bodies to their minds

—which wants so to acquire
a continuity, a place,
a demonstration that it must
be one's own sentence.

the ear

He cannot move the furniture
through that small aperture, yet
expects it must serve
used with reserve.

To wit, the company that comes
runs to be first in,
arranges what it can
within the man,

who (poor fool) bulges
with secrets he never divulges.

the skeleton

The element in which they live,
the shell going outward until
it never can end, formless,
seen on a clear night as stars,
the term of life given them
to come back to, down to,
and then to be in
themselves only, only skin.

the lion and the dog

Let who will think of what they will.
If the mind is made up, like an animal,
a lion to be suffered, a dog to pat,
action follows without conclusion

till all is stopped. The conclusion
is not variable, it is. From that
which was, then it, the lion if it is,
or dog, if it is, is not. It has

died to who thought of it, but comes
again there, to wherever that mind was,
or place, or circumstance being compound
of place, and time, now waiting but patient.

And all that is difficult, but difficult
not to think of, saying, lion, dog, thinking,
thinking patience, as an occasion of these,
but never having known them. But they come,

just as they came once, he thought, he
gave them each all that they were, lion,
but a word merely, and only a dog of sound.
All die equally. The mind is only there,

but here he is, thinking of them. They
are patient. What do they know? They know
nothing. They are not but as he thought.
But he knows nothing who thinks. They are.

the story

The tall woman wants the tall story
and sees from the tower, and saw more.

The history of acts is the form they make
toward one another as like waves they break.

The mind is coincident to any of several impinging
impregnated incidents like tomatoes ripening

—And the joke the friend told, incidentally, "the
young man who will accompany playing his silver balls,"

Did play them with a silver sound—and she
looked down and saw the small town from the far-off shore,

And the waves breaking and making up the ground
that ran from town to tower and then to her mind and back
again.

two times

1

It takes so long to look down,
the first time thinking it
would then and there either
shoot up or else drop off.

2

One hand on
the trigger one
hand on the hand.

a fragment

On the street I am met with constant hostility
and I would have finally nothing else around me,
except my children who are trained to love
and whom I intend to leave as relics of my intentions.